CW01582350

THIS HERBARIUM belongs to:

....

"Study nature, love nature, stay close to nature. It will never fail you."
– FRANK LLOYD WRIGHT

DISCOVER THE WONDERS OF NATURE AROUND YOU !

Use your herbarium journal to creatively explore and mindfully foster your connection with nature. Work with what is available around, sample different plants from the wild landscape and broaden your knowledge of surroundings. Play with every page: paste in pressings and pictures, record information, make notes and sketches.

GET INSPIRED TO STUDY NATURE AND LET IT GUIDE YOU THROUGH THE LEARNING PROCESS.

GATHER WHAT SPARKS YOUR WONDER

Venturing out into the wild, or even into your own backyard, to gather plants is so much fun! As you start looking around, you may get surprised with the variety of species in your area.

USE GLOVES when COLLECTING plants outside; some species can sting, or cause reactions with sensitive skin.

When gathering plants, try to harvest AS MANY PARTS AS POSSIBLE, including flowers, seeds, fruits, and roots.

Remember not to harvest plants in PLACES WHERE IT IS FORBIDDEN, i.e. National Parks. Avoid collecting any ENDANGERED or POISONOUS species.

Do a bit of research before collecting and get to know a little about your local flora.

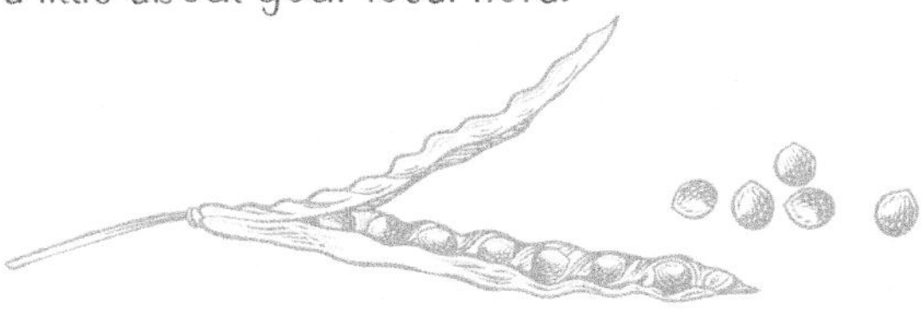

COMPILE YOUR HERBARIUM

Once your plants are dry, it's time to add them to your herbarium pages! Use the PRESSING SAMPLER PAGE to explore different methods of attaching your pressed specimens: rice glue, liquid glue, glue stick, paste, cello tape, etc.

Test what works best for various plant types.

Keep a piece of WAX PAPER (baking paper works too!) in between the pages while the glue is drying to prevent pages from sticking.

Use any leftover dry plants to create beautiful pressed compositions.

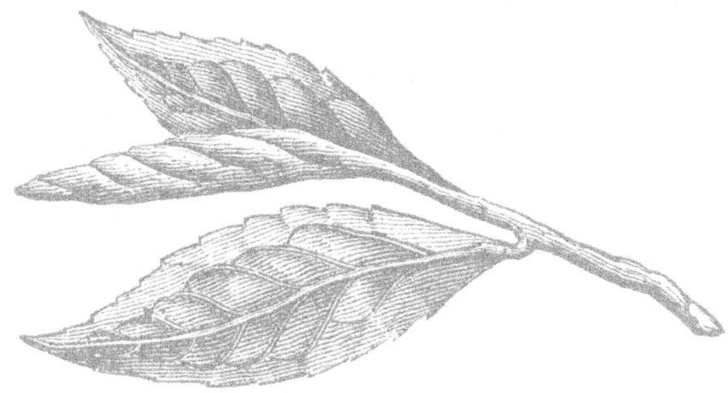

PRESS IT TO PRESERVE IT

Make sure all collected specimens are DRY to prevent mold while pressing. CLEAN OFF any moisture, dirt or bugs from your plants.

Open a thick, HEAVY BOOK and line the pages with a couple pieces of paper. Place the plant you wish to PRESS on the paper.

Carefully SPREAD YOUR PLANT out, so you can see all the parts of it. If the plant is large, bend and fold it to make it fit. You can dry several plants in the same book by spacing them few pages apart.

Once you have all the plants you wish to press in your book, close it, PLACE SOMETHING HEAVY ON TOP of it (i.e. more books) and set it aside for 7 to 10 DAYS to let the plants fully dry.

In the meantime, FILL YOUR HERBARIUM PAGES with botanical information and personal notes and sketches !

SPECIMEN COLLECTION LIST

Specimen No. 1 ....
Specimen No. 2 ....
Specimen No. 3 ....
Specimen No. 4 ....
Specimen No. 5 ....
Specimen No. 6 ....
Specimen No. 7 ....
Specimen No. 8 ....
Specimen No. 9 ....
Specimen No. 10 ....
Specimen No. 11 ....
Specimen No. 12 ....
Specimen No. 13 ....
Specimen No. 14 ....
Specimen No. 15 ....
Specimen No. 16 ....
Specimen No. 17 ....
Specimen No. 18 ....
Specimen No. 19 ....
Specimen No. 20 ....
Specimen No. 21 ....
Specimen No. 22 ....
Specimen No. 23 ....
Specimen No. 24 ....
Specimen No. 25 ....
Specimen No. 26 ....
Specimen No. 27 ....
Specimen No. 28 ....
Specimen No. 29 ....
Specimen No. 30 ....
Specimen No. 31 ....
Specimen No. 32 ....
Specimen No. 33 ....
Specimen No. 34 ....
Specimen No. 35 ....

PRESSING SAMPLER

LEAF

STEM

FLOWER

SEED

ROOT

OTHER

....

OTHER

....

OTHER

....

Explore different styles and methods of attaching various specimens to your herbarium pages.

Specimen No. ....

DATE: ....

PLANT INFO:

Common Name: ....

Scientific Name: ....

Plant Family: ....

Leaves: ....

Flowers: ....

Roots: ....

Stem/Trunk: ....

Area of Collection: ....

Other: ....

Habitat & Environment: ....

Effects & Usage: ....

NOTES

Specimen No. ....

DATE: ....

PLANT INFO:

Common Name: ....

Scientific Name: ....

Plant Family: ....

Leaves: ....

Flowers: ....

Roots: ....

Stem/Trunk: ....

Area of Collection: ....

Other: ....

Habitat & Environment: ....

....

....

Effects & Usage: ....

....

....

....

....

....

NOTES

Specimen No. ....

DATE: ....

PLANT INFO:

Common Name: ....

Scientific Name: ....

Plant Family: ....

Leaves: ....

Flowers: ....

Roots: ....

Stem/Trunk: ....

Area of Collection: ....

Other: ....

Habitat & Environment: ....

Effects & Usage: ....

NOTES

Specimen No. ....

DATE: ....

PLANT INFO:

Common Name: ....

Scientific Name: ....

Plant Family: ....

Leaves: ....

Flowers: ....

Roots: ....

Stem/Trunk: ....

Area of Collection: ....

Other: ....

Habitat & Environment: ....

Effects & Usage: ....

NOTES

Specimen No. ....

DATE: ....

PLANT INFO:

Common Name: ....

Scientific Name: ....

Plant Family: ....

Leaves: ....

Flowers: ....

Roots: ....

Stem/Trunk: ....

Area of Collection: ....

Other: ....

Habitat & Environment: ....

Effects & Usage: ....

NOTES

....

Specimen No. ....

DATE: ....

PLANT INFO:

Common Name: ....

Scientific Name: ....

Plant Family: ....

Leaves: ....

Flowers: ....

Roots: ....

Stem/Trunk: ....

Area of Collection: ....

Other: ....

Habitat & Environment: ....

....

....

Effects & Usage: ....

....

....

....

....

....

NOTES

Specimen No. ....

DATE: ....

PLANT INFO:

Common Name: ....

Scientific Name: ....

Plant Family: ....

Leaves: ....

Flowers: ....

Roots: ....

Stem/Trunk: ....

Area of Collection: ....

Other: ....

Habitat & Environment: ....

Effects & Usage: ....

NOTES

....

Specimen No. ....

DATE: ....

PLANT INFO:

Common Name: ....

Scientific Name: ....

Plant Family: ....

Leaves: ....

Flowers: ....

Roots: ....

Stem/Trunk: ....

Area of Collection: ....

Other: ....

Habitat & Environment: ....

Effects & Usage: ....

NOTES

Specimen No. ....

DATE: ....

PLANT INFO:

Common Name: ....

Scientific Name: ....

Plant Family: ....

Leaves: ....

Flowers: ....

Roots: ....

Stem/Trunk: ....

Area of Collection: ....

Other: ....

Habitat & Environment: ....

....

....

Effects & Usage: ....

....

....

....

....

....

NOTES

....

Specimen No. ....

DATE: ....

PLANT INFO:

Common Name: ....

Scientific Name: ....

Plant Family: ....

Leaves: ....

Flowers: ....

Roots: ....

Stem/Trunk: ....

Area of Collection: ....

Other: ....

Habitat & Environment: ....

Effects & Usage: ....

NOTES

Specimen No. ....

DATE: ....

PLANT INFO:

Common Name: .... Habitat & Environment: ....
Scientific Name: ....
Plant Family: ....
Leaves: .... Effects & Usage: ....
Flowers: ....
Roots: ....
Stem/Trunk: ....
Area of Collection: ....
Other: ....

NOTES

Specimen No. ....

DATE: ....

PLANT INFO:

Common Name: .... Habitat & Environment: ....

Scientific Name: ....

Plant Family: ....

Leaves: .... Effects & Usage: ....

Flowers: ....

Roots: ....

Stem/Trunk: ....

Area of Collection: ....

Other: ....

NOTES

Specimen No. ....

DATE: ....

PLANT INFO:

Common Name: .... Habitat & Environment: ....
Scientific Name: ....
Plant Family: ....
Leaves: .... Effects & Usage: ....
Flowers: ....
Roots: ....
Stem/Trunk: ....
Area of Collection: ....
Other: ....

NOTES

Specimen No. ....

DATE: ....

PLANT INFO:

Common Name: ....

Scientific Name: ....

Plant Family: ....

Leaves: ....

Flowers: ....

Roots: ....

Stem/Trunk: ....

Area of Collection: ....

Other: ....

Habitat & Environment: ....

Effects & Usage: ....

NOTES

Specimen No. ....

DATE: ....

PLANT INFO:

Common Name: ....

Scientific Name: ....

Plant Family: ....

Leaves: ....

Flowers: ....

Roots: ....

Stem/Trunk: ....

Area of Collection: ....

Other: ....

Habitat & Environment: ....

Effects & Usage: ....

NOTES

Specimen No. ....

DATE: ....

PLANT INFO:

Common Name: ....

Scientific Name: ....

Plant Family: ....

Leaves: ....

Flowers: ....

Roots: ....

Stem/Trunk: ....

Area of Collection: ....

Other: ....

Habitat & Environment: ....

Effects & Usage: ....

NOTES

Specimen No. ....

DATE: ....

PLANT INFO:

Common Name: ....
Scientific Name: ....
Plant Family: ....
Leaves: ....
Flowers: ....
Roots: ....
Stem/Trunk: ....
Area of Collection: ....
Other: ....

Habitat & Environment: ....

Effects & Usage: ....

NOTES

Specimen No. ....

DATE: ....

PLANT INFO:

Common Name: ....
Scientific Name: ....
Plant Family: ....
Leaves: ....
Flowers: ....
Roots: ....
Stem/Trunk: ....
Area of Collection: ....
Other: ....

Habitat & Environment: ....
....
....
Effects & Usage: ....
....
....
....
....
....

NOTES

Specimen No. ....

DATE: ....

PLANT INFO:

Common Name: ....

Scientific Name: ....

Plant Family: ....

Leaves: ....

Flowers: ....

Roots: ....

Stem/Trunk: ....

Area of Collection: ....

Other: ....

Habitat & Environment: ....

Effects & Usage: ....

NOTES

Specimen No. ....

DATE: ....

PLANT INFO:

Common Name: ....

Scientific Name: ....

Plant Family: ....

Leaves: ....

Flowers: ....

Roots: ....

Stem/Trunk: ....

Area of Collection: ....

Other: ....

Habitat & Environment: ....

....

....

Effects & Usage: ....

....

....

....

....

....

NOTES

Specimen No. ....

DATE: ....

PLANT INFO:

Common Name: ....

Scientific Name: ....

Plant Family: ....

Leaves: ....

Flowers: ....

Roots: ....

Stem/Trunk: ....

Area of Collection: ....

Other: ....

Habitat & Environment: ....

....

....

Effects & Usage: ....

....

....

....

....

....

NOTES

....

Specimen No. ....

DATE: ....

PLANT INFO:

Common Name: .... Habitat & Environment: ....

Scientific Name: ....

Plant Family: ....

Leaves: .... Effects & Usage: ....

Flowers: ....

Roots: ....

Stem/Trunk: ....

Area of Collection: ....

Other: ....

NOTES

Specimen No. ....

DATE: ....

PLANT INFO:

Common Name: ....

Scientific Name: ....

Plant Family: ....

Leaves: ....

Flowers: ....

Roots: ....

Stem/Trunk: ....

Area of Collection: ....

Other: ....

Habitat & Environment: ....

Effects & Usage: ....

NOTES

....

Specimen No. ....

DATE: ....

PLANT INFO:

Common Name: ....

Scientific Name: ....

Plant Family: ....

Leaves: ....

Flowers: ....

Roots: ....

Stem/Trunk: ....

Area of Collection: ....

Other: ....

Habitat & Environment: ....

Effects & Usage: ....

NOTES

Specimen No. ....

DATE: ....

PLANT INFO:

Common Name: ....

Scientific Name: ....

Plant Family: ....

Leaves: ....

Flowers: ....

Roots: ....

Stem/Trunk: ....

Area of Collection: ....

Other: ....

Habitat & Environment: ....

Effects & Usage: ....

NOTES

Specimen No. ....

DATE: ....

PLANT INFO:

Common Name: ....

Scientific Name: ....

Plant Family: ....

Leaves: ....

Flowers: ....

Roots: ....

Stem/Trunk: ....

Area of Collection: ....

Other: ....

Habitat & Environment: ....

....

....

Effects & Usage: ....

....

....

....

....

....

NOTES

Specimen No. ....

DATE: ....

PLANT INFO:

Common Name: ....

Scientific Name: ....

Plant Family: ....

Leaves: ....

Flowers: ....

Roots: ....

Stem/Trunk: ....

Area of Collection: ....

Other: ....

Habitat & Environment: ....

Effects & Usage: ....

NOTES

....

Specimen No. ....

DATE:

PLANT INFO:

Common Name:

Scientific Name:

Plant Family:

Leaves:

Flowers:

Roots:

Stem/Trunk:

Area of Collection:

Other:

Habitat & Environment:

Effects & Usage:

NOTES

Specimen No. ....

DATE: ....

PLANT INFO:

Common Name: ....

Scientific Name: ....

Plant Family: ....

Leaves: ....

Flowers: ....

Roots: ....

Stem/Trunk: ....

Area of Collection: ....

Other: ....

Habitat & Environment: ....

Effects & Usage: ....

NOTES

Specimen No. ....

DATE: ....

PLANT INFO:

Common Name: ....

Scientific Name: ....

Plant Family: ....

Leaves: ....

Flowers: ....

Roots: ....

Stem/Trunk: ....

Area of Collection: ....

Other: ....

Habitat & Environment: ....

....

....

Effects & Usage: ....

....

....

....

....

....

NOTES

Specimen No. ....

DATE: ....

PLANT INFO:

Common Name: ....

Scientific Name: ....

Plant Family: ....

Leaves: ....

Flowers: ....

Roots: ....

Stem/Trunk: ....

Area of Collection: ....

Other: ....

Habitat & Environment: ....

Effects & Usage: ....

NOTES

Specimen No. ....

DATE: ....

PLANT INFO:

Common Name: ....

Scientific Name: ....

Plant Family: ....

Leaves: ....

Flowers: ....

Roots: ....

Stem/Trunk: ....

Area of Collection: ....

Other: ....

Habitat & Environment: ....

Effects & Usage: ....

NOTES

Specimen No. ....

DATE: ....

PLANT INFO:

Common Name: ....

Scientific Name: ....

Plant Family: ....

Leaves: ....

Flowers: ....

Roots: ....

Stem/Trunk: ....

Area of Collection: ....

Other: ....

Habitat & Environment: ....

....

....

Effects & Usage: ....

....

....

....

....

....

NOTES

Specimen No. ....

DATE: ....

PLANT INFO:

Common Name: ....
Scientific Name: ....
Plant Family: ....
Leaves: ....
Flowers: ....
Roots: ....
Stem/Trunk: ....
Area of Collection: ....
Other: ....

Habitat & Environment: ....

Effects & Usage: ....

NOTES

Specimen No. ....

DATE: ....

PLANT INFO:

Common Name: .... Habitat & Environment: ....
Scientific Name: ....
Plant Family: ....
Leaves: .... Effects & Usage: ....
Flowers: ....
Roots: ....
Stem/Trunk: ....
Area of Collection: ....
Other: ....

NOTES

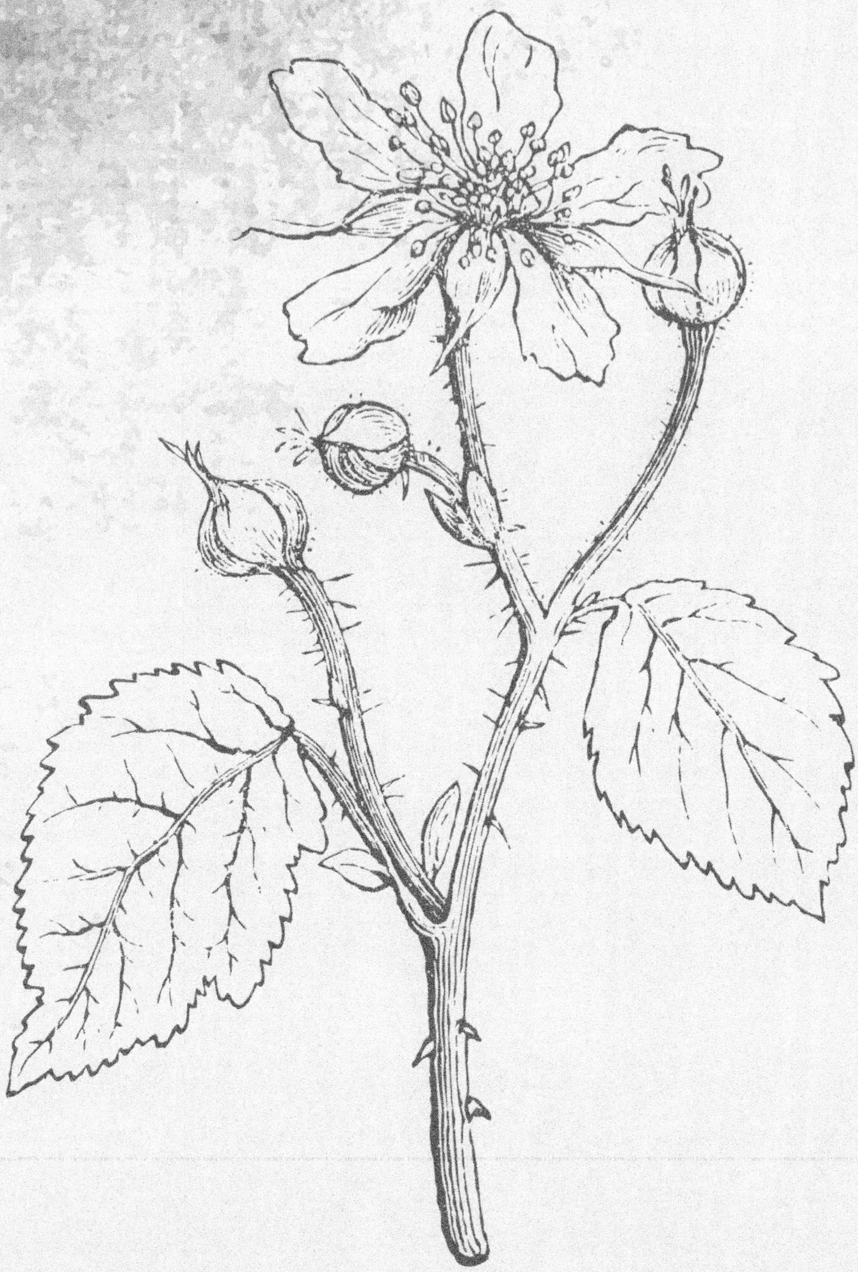

HERBARIUM: PRESSED NATURE JOURNAL

For Discovering, Collecting & Identifying Plants, Leaves And Flowers

Outdoor Explorers Activity Book Log For Kids & Adults

© 2020 Ava Boone. All Rights Reserved

Illustrations by Freepik

Printed in Great Britain
by Amazon

65928529R00059